Sociology in Pictures Research Methods
Teacher's Guide
Michael Haralambos
with Wendy Hope

Contents

Published by Collins Educational
An imprint of HarperCollins Publishers, 77-85 Fulham Palace Road, Hammersmith, London W6 8JB

© Michael Haralambos, 2012
10 9 8 7 6 5 4 3 2 1
ISBN 978-0-00-748283-2

British Library Cataloguing in Publication Data.
A catalogue record for this publication is available from the British Library.

Typography and design by John A Collins and Derek Baker

Printed and bound in the UK by www.waringcollins.com

PARTICIPANT OBSERVATION

QUESTIONS AND ANSWERS

Q1   Look at the top two pictures. Why do you think the young men are laughing at Sudhir?

A   To tick a box in response to a complex question about your life appears ridiculous. Some of the alternative responses also seem ridiculous. For example, to offer the possibility that to be 'black and poor' might be seen as 'very good' shows just how ignorant the researcher is. Sudhir appears naïve and stupid to be wandering around the streets alone. This is a dangerous area, especially for a young middle-class academic.

Q2   Why did JT suggest that Sudhir should 'hang out'?

A   So he could learn about their way of life which his questionnaire suggests that he knows little or nothing about. By hanging out, he might learn to ask questions which are relevant to the lives of those he is studying.

Q3   Why didn't the gang like interviews and questionnaires?

A   • Because they usually indicate ignorance of their way of life.
     • Because they are sometimes used by figures in authority such as police and social workers who gang members distrust.
     • Because the questions reflect the concerns of those who ask them.
     • Because gang members think their answers might be used against them.

Q4   What has Sudhir learned about participant observation?

A   As the thought bubble indicates, to look, listen and stay in the background is the best way to get results. Don't ask questions, don't intrude and appear to mind your own business.

BACKGROUND

Sudhir Venkatesh is the son of Indian migrants. He grew up in the suburbs of southern California. He had no experience of low-income black neighbourhoods before starting his fieldwork. His research was conducted in high-rise projects (social housing), in one of the poorest areas of Chicago with high rates of crime, unemployment and welfare. He is now Professor of Sociology at Columbia University in New York.

GAINING ENTRY

QUESTIONS AND ANSWERS

Q1 *Briefly comment on the reactions of the gang members on Day 1*

A Some of the gang see Sudhir as a possible threat as the gun and knife suggest. They clearly want nothing to do with him as their statements indicate. Since their activities are illegal, they are very suspicious of strangers.

Some of the gang see him as a source of amusement and, as such, probably harmless and even 'crazy' as the comment on Day 2 indicated.

Those who are observed try to make sense of a participant observer and to explain their behaviour. One gang member sees Sudhir as a member of a rival Mexican gang. This provides an explanation for Sudhir's presence – he is spy – and his complexion appears Mexican.

Q2 *Why is it important to gain JT's support?*

A JT is the gang leader. His word carries weight and can influence the gang. Gaining his support is vital for the success of Sudhir's research.

Q3 *What does Day 3 indicate?*

A Sudhir has gained entry. He is relaxed and smiling as are the gang members who appear to have welcomed him into their group.

BACKGROUND

Here are some quotations from Sudhir's book *Gang Leader For A Day*. They indicate why participant observation was a particularly suitable method for his research.

- 'I had no experience whatsoever in an urban ghetto.'
- 'I was an outsider looking at life from the inside.'
- 'As alien as I was to these folks, they were just as alien to me.'
- 'They saw me as a little naïve and more than a little loopy. Looking back, I can't say they were wrong.'
- 'I realised that if I truly wanted to understand the complicated lives of black youth in inner-city Chicago, I had only one good option: to accept JT's counsel and hang out with people.'
- 'JT let me into a new world with a level of trust I had no reason to expect.'

ACTING NORMALLY

QUESTIONS AND ANSWERS

Q1 *To what extent do a) the boys and b) the teachers, appear to have acted normally during the research?*

A a) As Hargreaves notes, his presence at the back of the classroom caused changes in the boys' behaviour. They were aware of his presence, they turned round to stare at him and did not pay attention to the teacher. However, by Day 5 the boys appeared to have got used to him and seemed to be behaving normally.

b) Hargreaves believed that many of the teachers behaved normally when he was observing them. However, he admits that it is 'difficult to check on the extent of the changes my presence produced'. The boys tell a somewhat different story. In their view, at least some of the teachers changed their behaviour. They 'put on a show' in Hargreaves' presence, being over-friendly and uncharacteristically kind and pleasant.

Q2 *Why are participant observers so concerned that those they observe act normally?*

A Researchers use participant observation to observe people acting normally and naturally in their everyday social settings. If their behaviour is changed by the presence of an observer, then the whole point of this research method is lost. The researcher's presence will have created an abnormal setting and, as a result, they will not be acting normally.

BACKGROUND

David Hargreaves spent a year observing the behaviour of teachers and students in a boys' secondary modern school. He already had three years teaching experience and spent a third of his time actually teaching in the school. He saw this as helping him to gain acceptance, particularly from teachers. Here are some of his comments on his choice of participant observation.

'The method of participant observation leads the investigator to accept the role within the social situation he studies: he participates as a member of the group as well as observing it. In theory, this direct participation in the group life permits an easy entrance into the social situation by reducing the resistance of group members; decreases the extent to which the investigator disturbs the 'natural' situation; and permits the investigator to experience and observe the group's norms, values, conflicts and pressures, which (over a long period) cannot be hidden from someone playing an in-group role.'

STREET CORNER SOCIETY

QUESTIONS AND ANSWERS

Q1 *If you know little about those you are studying, why is it important just to just listen?*

A If you are basing your research on interviews or questionnaires, you ask the questions. But are those the questions relevant to those you are studying? Do they reflect their concerns and priorities? You can't be sure. However, if you gain their trust and participate in their daily lives, you have a far better choice of seeing the world through their eyes and of finding out what matters to them. This is what Whyte found as he 'sat and listened'.

Q2 *Why should participant observers be careful about asking questions?*

A To some extent, participant observers become a member of the group they observe. As such, they must be aware of the norms of the group and behave accordingly. In particular, they must avoid asking questions which might be seen as intrusive, embarrassing, annoying , offensive, or upsetting, especially in front of other people.

Asking personal questions in public may antagonise people and spoil the observer's relationship with those they are studying. This can be seen by Whyte's question to the gambler. It might result, in Doc's words, in people 'clamming up on you'. And this is the last thing a researcher wants.

Q3 *One of the dangers of participant observation is influencing the behaviour of those being observed. Why is this a concern?*

A One of the strengths of participant observation is the opportunity to see people behaving normally in their everyday settings. If their behaviour is influenced by the researcher, then to some extent, they will not behave normally. As Doc, the gang leader said, Whyte's presence 'slowed me up plenty'.

Q4 *Immersed in a group for a long time – 3½ years in Whyte's case – may lead observers to take things for granted. Why is this a problem?*

A If the researchers become, in Whyte's words, 'almost a non-observing participant', they may not notice important aspect of behaviour. They may fail to record everyday activity because they take it for granted.

BACKGROUND

William Whyte was a young middle-class white American with a strong commitment to social reform. He studied a working-class Italian American gang in a low-income district of Boston. The observer and the observed came from very different backgrounds. Doc, the gang leader, sponsored Whyte and reassured gang members that Whyte could be trusted. Doc also 'became in a very real sense, a collaborator in the research', discussing 'ideas and observations'.

Whyte's research is regarded as a classic example of participant observation.

OBSERVATIONS IN CONTEXT

QUESTIONS AND ANSWERS

Q1 For part of his research, Jason Ditton kept the real reason for working at Wellbread Bakery a secret.

a) Why might this have helped his research?

b) What ethical problems does this raise?

A　a) Because Ditton was investigating fiddles, he needed to gain the workers' trust. If they saw him as a fellow worker, he was more likely to do so. If they saw him as an outsider, they may not have talked openly and honestly to him, especially if they saw him as a researcher who might be reporting back to management.

b) Today, most researchers would see secrecy as unethical. Research ethics state that people should be told they are taking part in a study and what the study is about. Many researchers would argue that by keeping his real reasons for being at Wellbread secret, Ditton was lying to the workers.

Q2 Participant observation provides an opportunity to observe what people say and do in different contexts. Judging from Liebow's study, why is this important?

A　People behave differently in different contexts. They say one thing in one situation and another in another situation. To understand how they see themselves, how they picture the world they live in and why they act in apparently contradictory ways, it is important to observe them in different situations. Participant observation provides an opportunity to make these observations.

This can be seen from Liebow's research. On the street corner the men are boasting about their sexual prowess. They blame their failure as husbands on their success as 'macho men'. However, in a different context – a bar and a few drinks – the pain and sadness of a broken relationship finds expression. Observation of both contexts is necessary to understand the men's behaviour.

BACKGROUND

Jason Ditton had previously worked at the bakery as a student during his holidays. As a result, he already knew most of the men and had no trouble getting accepted. He describes himself as an 'undercover participant observer' and admits his findings were 'deceitfully gathered'. He then became 'partially open although I never fully declared that I was chiefly interested in fiddling'.

Elliot Liebow told the men he observed what he was doing. His parents were Jewish immigrants from Eastern Europe. He was born and raised in a predominantly black neighbourhood in Washington D.C. and felt comfortable mixing with African Americans. However, he admits that his colour 'absolutely relegated me to the status of outsider – they saw, first of all, a white man'.

Liebow observed the men in a variety of contexts – on the street corner, in their apartments, listening to music at Nancy's Place, going to parties, crap games and drinking in bars. He focused on 'what they said, what they did, and the contexts in which they said and did them'.

ETHNOGRAPHY

QUESTIONS AND ANSWERS

Q1 *What is Malinowski's view of ethnography?*

A To see the world through the eyes of those he observed, to understand their point of view.

Q2 *Malinowski spent considerable time studying gardening on the Trobriand Islands. Why?*

A Gardening was very important to the Trobriand men – they spent half their lives gardening. Its importance is also reflected in the existence of specialised gardening magicians who conduct ceremonies to help the crops grow. Gardening is not just about food. It is also about social status. A man's standing in the community is based partly on his gardening ability. A good crop is admired and brings praise to the grower. Malinowski saw his job as an ethnographer to see gardening through the eyes of the Trobriand men and the community as a whole.

BACKGROUND

Bronislaw Malinowski (1884 – 1942) was born in Poland, became a British citizen, and is regarded as one of the founding fathers of ethnography. He argued that to understand society required a knowledge of its various parts and how they fit together. And the best way of doing this is as a participant observer, looking at the entire way of life of a community.

A flavour of Malinowski's research is contained in the following quotation.

'Soon after I had established myself in the Trobriand Islands, I began to take part in village life, to look forward to the important or festive events, to take personal interest in the gossip and the developments of the small village occurrences.'

'As I went on my morning walk through the village, I could see intimate details of family life, of toilet, cooking , taking of meals; I could see the arrangements for the day's work, people starting on their errands, or groups of men and women busy at some manufacturing tasks. Quarrels, jokes, family scenes, events usually trivial, sometimes dramatic but always significant, formed the atmosphere of my daily life, as well as theirs.'

Note: Lengthy studies based on participant observation are often called ethnographies – for example, those of Sudhir Venkatesh, William Whyte and Elliot Liebow.

QUESTIONS AND ANSWERS

Q1 *Suggest the advantages and disadvantages of a) structured interviews and b) unstructured interviews.*

A **Structured interviews – advantages**
- Everybody is asked the same questions so their responses can be directly compared – they are not responding differently due to different wording of the same question.
- It is relatively easy to quantify the responses – put them into a numerical form. For example, '75 % agreed with the statement that…'
- Structured interviews are particularly suitable for simple, straightforward 'factual' information such as the interviewee's gender, age and occupation.

Structured interviews – disadvantages
- Limitations are placed on the interviewee's responses – for example, choosing between fixed alternatives as in 'yes' or 'no' answers.
- Interviewees have little opportunity to discuss and qualify their answers.
- Interviewees are unable to introduce or develop issues which are important to them.

Unstructured interviews – advantages
- Opportunity for interviewees to answer questions in their own way and in their own words.
- Opportunity to bring in and develop their own concerns and priorities.
- Unstructured interviews are particularly suitable for sensitive topics, shades of meaning, attitudes and opinions. They can provide more in-depth and 'richer' data.

Unstructured interviews – disadvantages
- The chances of the interviewer influencing the responses of the interviewee are greater.
- Comparison of the data from different interviews is difficult. Unstructured interviews can develop in all sorts of directions.

Q2 *Briefly suggest the advantages and disadvantages of different interview styles and techniques – rapport, assertiveness and feminist.*

A **Rapport** If a friendly and understanding relationship is developed by the interviewer, then the interviewee will be more likely to cooperate and do their best to fully answer the questions. However, this may lead to the interviewee giving answers which they think the interviewer wants.

Assertiveness Becker argues that taking a more direct and assertive approach may result in more honest and frank answers. However, this may lead interviewees to see the interviewer as aggressive and they may withdraw their cooperation.

Feminist Female interviewees may be more open with a female interviewer. They may feel that shared gender means greater sympathy and understanding, especially if they are treated as an equal. As a result, they may reveal much more about their views and feelings. However, some researchers argue that if the interviewer is understanding and sympathetic, then their gender shouldn't make much difference.

INTERVIEW EFFECTS

QUESTIONS AND ANSWERS

Q1 *Look at the top two pictures. Suggest how the settings and the interviewers might affect the interviewee's responses.*

A   In the first picture the interviewer looks grumpy. His language and the setting are formal. The interviewee doesn't like the look of him. As a result, her responses will tend to be short and to the point. She probably won't volunteer additional information and she'll want to get the interview over as soon as possible.

In the second picture, the setting is informal – arm chairs, cheerful fire, coffee – and the interviewer is friendly and smiling as she greets the student. It's woman to woman, which might put the student more at ease. And her reaction is, 'She seems nice'. This suggests the student will be forthcoming, she will volunteer information and will enjoy the interview.

Q2 *Briefly explain how the interviewees' definition of the interviewer in Parker's study might affect their responses.*

A   Perceptions of the interviewer's age, expertise and experience appear to influence the responses he received. In the first picture, the older man talks down to the 'young man' who he sees as a 'novice' and a junior. The older man will probably keep his responses simple and may be patronising.

In the second picture, the interviewee is young, he sees the interviewer as an 'expert' and wonders why he is asking for the opinion of someone who is 'only an office junior'. As a result, he will probably feel ill at ease and his responses will be minimal.

In the third picture, those involved are a similar age. The interviewer appears to be used a confidante by someone who needs to get things off her chest.

BACKGROUND

It is useful to think of interviews as interaction situations which share many of the aspects found in all situations. People define each other in terms of the other's social characteristics – nationality, ethnicity, gender, social class, age group – the other's personality – shy/outgoing, sympathetic/unsympathetic, friendly/ unfriendly and so on. They respond to settings – formal/informal, cold and official/warm and personal. These and many other factors affect responses in interaction situations in general and interviews in particular.

Martin Parker conducted 100 interviews with 74 people in 3 different organisations. As shown in the pictures, he was given 3 main identities. Senior management tended to refer to him as a novice, calling him 'lad' or 'son' because of his age – he was under 30 – and his lack of expertise and knowledge. He had a more equal relationship with younger, lower status employees around his own age, who tended to treat him as a confidante. As one said, 'It's nice to have somebody to talk to and moan to'. The third identity as an expert was given to him by staff who were very junior. These interviews 'were the least fruitful. I often felt my interviewees were simply rehearsing things they felt I wanted to hear.'

QUESTIONS AND ANSWERS

Q1 *Use the idea of social desirability to explain the answers of the interviewees in the two pictures.*

A Social desirability is the tendency of people to present themselves in a positive light in the presence of others. This means they will project aspects of their behaviour which are generally seen as desirable and hide aspects of behaviour seen as undesirable. Some people see regular church attendance as socially desirable and may well exaggerate the frequency of their attendance. This may explain the response of the interviewee in the first picture.

In the second picture the woman conceals the fact that she has taken cocaine in the past year. She is aware that many people disapprove of illegal drug use, particularly the use of 'hard' drugs such as cocaine. She pictures the negative stereotype of the regular cocaine user which she thinks the interviewer holds. As a result, she lies and says no to his question.

Q2 *Suggest another reason for the woman's denial of cocaine use.*

A Cocaine is an illegal drug and as a 'hard' drug is taken particularly seriously by the authorities. Because of this, denial makes sense because of the possible consequences of admitting to using cocaine.

BACKGROUND

There have been a number of studies in the USA which show that surveys of church attendance using face-to-face structured interviews, telephone interviews and self-completion questionnaires, all exaggerate attendance. Actual attendance is usually around half reported attendance. The reason for this seems to be social desirability bias.

The Chicago study of cocaine use was based on a random sample of 18 to 40 year olds. They were guaranteed anonymity. The researchers argue that social desirability effects are the main reason for under-reporting . However, as noted above, despite the promise of confidentiality, some people may have denied use for fear of information reaching the authorities.

QUESTIONS AND ANSWERS

Q1 *Look at the three interviews. Suggest reasons for the boys' responses in each case.*

A a) In the first interview, the boy sees the interview as threatening. The situation is formal and he is being interviewed by an adult he does not know. His answers are minimal so as little as possible can be held against him. The fact that the interviewer is white may make the boy even more defensive.

b) In the second interview, the boy's behaviour is similar to that in the first interview. In this case, the interviewer is black, so skin colour does not appear to be a significant factor. Again it appears that the formal situation and an unknown adult account for the boy's response.

c) In the third interview, the situation is informal, the boy's best friend is present, they are sitting on the floor munching potato crisps, and the boy has already met the interviewer. The boy defines the situation as friendly, he no longer feels threatened by the interviewer, and is now at ease. His response is transformed and he gives a detailed and articulate description of the toy plane.

Q2 *Briefly comment on the suitability of these interviews for assessing the boys' linguistic skills.*

A The first two interviews are unsuitable for assessing the boys' linguistic skills. The short, inadequate answers reflect the boys' definition of the situation rather than their verbal ability. As the third interview indicates, the monosyllabic child has become an articulate young person. Clearly, to assess young people's linguistic skills, they must be interviewed in a context where they feel at ease.

BACKGROUND

This is an important study. Some educationalists blamed the low attainment of many children (particularly black children) from low-income families, on the inadequacies of their language skills. The study questions this view. The researcher, William Labov, states, 'It means that the social situation is the most powerful determinant of verbal behaviour and that an adult must enter into the right social relation with a child if they want to find out what that child can do.'

QUESTIONNAIRES

QUESTIONS AND ANSWERS

Q1 *Reconstruct suitable questions to replace those given in the first five pictures.*

A   1. Briefly outline your views on abortion.

   2. What do you think about keeping animals in zoos?

   3. How often do you drink coffee?

☐	Once a day	☐	Four times a day
☐	Twice a day	☐	Five time a day
☐	Three times a day	☐	More than five times a day

   4. McDonald's are found in nearly every town and city. Do you agree?

   5. Should people's personal views be taken into account when considering them for a job in a nursery school?

☐	Yes	☐	No

Q2 *From your list in Question 1, select one question which is particularly suitable for a questionnaire and one which is better suited to an unstructured interview. Give reasons for your choices.*

A   The question on coffee drinking is particularly suited to a questionnaire because it is clear and simple and offers specific alternatives.

   The question on abortion is probably better suited to an unstructured interview because abortion is a complex issue and answers will probably require ifs, buts and maybes.

QUESTIONS AND ANSWERS

Q1 *Suggest reasons for the differing responses of the manager of the Sunrise Motel.*

A In the 1930s, when this study was conducted, there was considerable prejudice and discrimination in the USA against Chinese Americans. Discrimination was not illegal at the time.

Face-to-face interaction, questionnaires and telephone calls are different situations and can result in different responses. There are many factors involved in social interaction which influence responses – for example, dress, demeanour and facial expression. Responding to a postal questionnaire or a phone call does not involve many of these factors. If the manager assumes the query is from a member of the white majority, then he might well say that the motel won't accept Chinese guests for fear of losing customers. However, a face-to-face interaction with a young Chinese couple asking for a room is a different situation which produces a different response.

Q2 *Suggest reasons for false memories.*

A People readily respond to suggestions when asked to recall events, especially when the suggestions seem reasonable and the events occurred many years ago. Bugs Bunny is a cartoon character and for many people he would not seem out of place in Disneyland.

Children are particularly suggestible, especially when faced with an adult interviewer. They were presented with a list of videos, some of which had been invented for the study. When asked to select those they had seen, they assumed that all the videos were real and said that they had seen some of the invented ones.

BACKGROUND

Richard LaPiere's classic study *Attitudes vs Actions* questions the view that people's actions will reflect their attitudes as reported in questionnaires. Faced with a well-spoken, well-mannered, well-dressed, young, attractive Chinese couple requesting a room in a motel is very different from responding to a phone call or written question about whether the motel would accept Chinese guests. This is an important study because some researchers assume that attitudes, as measured by questionnaires, will usually be translated into behaviour.

Psychologists have conducted many experiments into false memory syndrome. They have shown that false memories can be fairly easily implanted, to the point where people are convinced that they are true.

SAMPLING METHODS

QUESTIONS AND ANSWERS

Q1 *Why is it important that samples be representative?*

A A representative sample reflects or represents the group as a whole. For example, it represents the proportion of age groups or gender groups in the population as a whole. If the sample is representative, then findings from the survey should be applicable to the group as a whole – the findings can be generalised.

Q2 *Why use simple random samples?*

A Simple random samples are not necessarily representative. For example, if the sample is intended to represent college students, it might include mostly female students. This can happen when the sample is randomly drawn even though females make up only half the student population.

However, a simple random sample prevents the researcher from selecting a sample which provides a result which fits their theory, supports their hypothesis, that gives them what they expect and what they want.

Q3 *Why is a stratified random sample likely to be more representative than a simple random sample?*

A A stratified random sample reflects the population as a whole in terms of one or more 'strata' such as age, gender, ethnicity, class. This will probably produce a more representative sample than simple random sampling. For example, if the aim is to reflect gender divisions in the UK, then 51 % of the sample will be randomly selected from the female stratum and 49 % from the male stratum. In terms of gender, the sample will reflect the proportion of females and males in the population as a whole.

Q4 *How representative are quota samples, snowball samples and volunteer samples likely to be?*

A **Quota samples** Although quota samples may reflect aspects of the general population, the sample is not randomly selected. The researcher selects people to fill their quota – they might choose friendly, better dressed people. Second, those available to fill the quota are unlikely to be representative of the general population. For example, stopping people on the street during working hours will exclude many people in employment.

Snowball samples are unlikely to produce representative samples as the sample members are not randomly selected. The sample relies on personal contacts and recommendations.

Volunteer samples are unlikely to be representative because the sample members select themselves. Those who volunteer may have a particular reason for doing so – they may have a grievance to express, a strongly held point of view to air, or simply nothing better to do. In each case, they may not be representative of the population as a whole.

QUESTIONS AND ANSWERS

Q1 Briefly explain the response in each of the pictures.

A   **Picture 1** Can't be bothered, no interest, probably sees it as junk mail.

Picture 2 Probably agreed to complete the questionnaire when it was delivered. Details of the research have already been given and he thinks it is important and interesting.

Picture 3 As he says, his English isn't good enough to understand and complete the questionnaire.

Picture 4 A low response rate often occurs when the questionnaire or interview concerns hurtful events – such as rape and incest – which people have experienced. They don't want painful memories to surface.

Picture 5 The parents are probably embarrassed about their overweight child and their failure to control his weight. They may well regard the researcher as an interfering busybody, which may explain their refusal to participate in the survey.

Picture 6 The response rate is low because many offenders may have had particularly negative experiences of probation. Even those who did take part may have had negative experiences as the picture indicates.

Picture 7 Reasons for low response are given in the caption – death , emigration, failure to trace and refusal to continue participation. Other reasons include illness, in prison, working away from home, experiencing some personal tragedy.

Q2 What are the problems of a low response rate?

A   It may result in an unrepresentative sample as those who do not respond might differ in important respects from those who do. For example, they may be younger or from a particular ethnic group or social class. In such cases this may result in an unrepresentative sample. And if the results of the research are used by policy makers, this can have serious consequences – for example, the Department of Health's study of children's weight.

BACKGROUND

In some cases it is still possible to measure the response rate – for example the proportion who did not respond in a simple random sample. In other cases it is not possible. For example, there is no way of measuring the response rate from a volunteer sample. How many people had seen the request for volunteers and decided not to respond?

TYPES OF DATA

QUESTIONS AND ANSWERS

Q1 *Suggest advantages and disadvantages of a) quantitative data and b) qualitative data.*

A **a) Quantitative data** Data in the form of numbers means that measurement and statistical analysis are possible. The data can be used to indicate the strength of possible relationships between various factors, for example, between social class and educational attainment and between age and internet use.

Because quantitative data is often relatively cheap and easy to collect – much of it comes from questionnaire surveys – samples are usually larger than studies producing qualitative data. And this also means that repeat surveys are more frequent. These can show trends over time as indicated by the statistics on women in higher education, smoking and marriage.

Data that can be effectively quantified often comes from simple, straightforward questions. For example, How old are you? Where do you live? Do you smoke? What is your occupation? Quantifying more complex issues is often less successful – for example, quantifying views on marriage, divorce, religion, and private education.

b) Qualitative data Qualitative data is often seen as richer and having greater depth than the numbers provided by quantitative data. It can be argued that the picture of people's lives provided by a qualitative method such as participant observation gives greater insight than answers to a questionnaire. And that a discussion of people's views and opinions in an unstructured interview gives greater depth than ticking boxes or giving short answers in a questionnaire.

However, qualitative methods are often more time-consuming, more expensive and based on smaller samples than quantitative methods. And data from qualitative research is often much more difficult to quantify and compare. In a questionnaire survey, people are responding to the same questions, which make it easier to compare the data. In a participant observation study, the data is much more dependent on the observational and interpretivist skills of the researcher. As a result, it is difficult to directly compare the results of two or more such studies.

BACKGROUND

Some researchers swear by quantitative data and reject descriptive and supposedly in-depth qualitative data. From their viewpoint, if you can't measure it, it's not worth having. At the other extreme, some researchers reject number crunching and look to what they see as the truth and validity of qualitative data and methods. Increasingly, sociologists are recognising the strengths and weaknesses of both types of data and the methods used to collect them. This can be seen from the growing support for 'mixed methods' research.

EXPERIMENTS

QUESTIONS AND ANSWERS

Q1 Why do some researchers use laboratories to conduct experiments?

A Laboratories give them control over what happens. They can control the variables (factors which might vary). In the pictures, variables such as lighting and temperature are kept the same for all participants. The only difference is the noise level. If there are differences in memory which correlate with differences in noise level, then this suggests that noise affects memory.

Researchers often use laboratory experiments to test hypotheses – in this case the hypothesis is: Noise affects memory.

Q2 Suggest problems with data from laboratory experiments.

A Laboratories are artificial environments. As a result, people might behave very differently in a laboratory than they would in the outside world. The tasks they are asked to perform in a laboratory experiment are also artificial. As the woman in the picture says – 'It is a meaningless task'. For these reasons, critics argue that behaviour in the laboratory does not necessarily reflect behaviour in the 'real' world.

Q3 How is the Hawthorne effect produced?

A The Hawthorne effect is the behaviour that results from people's awareness that they are part of an experiment and are being observed. As the experiment at the Hawthorne Works indicates, this awareness can be very powerful – it overrides the possible effect of changes in the working environment, such as increases and decreases in temperature and lighting.

BACKGROUND

The Hawthorne effect was first discovered in the 1920s during a study at the Hawthorne Works of the Western Electricity Company in Chicago – hence its name. The researchers were examining factors affecting productivity. The results didn't seem to make sense. For example, productivity rose whether the temperature and lighting were turned up or down. The only factor which appeared to make sense of these results was the fact that the workers knew they were being observed – the Hawthorne effect.

QUESTIONS AND ANSWERS

Q1 *Correlation does not necessarily indicate causation. Briefly explain this statement.*

A Just because two things are found together it doesn't mean that one causes the other.

Q2 *The correlation in Pictures 1 and 2 is probably non-causal. Why?*

A First, the correlation apparently only occurred for 12 years after World War Two. If it were causal, it should have continued. Second, it is very unlikely that stork fertility and human fertility are causally related. It stretches the imagination to assume that storks influence human behaviour in this way and/or vice versa.

Q3 *Pictures 3 and 4 present a simple example of a correlation caused by a third factor. Here is a more complex example. There is a correlation between working class people and crime.*
a) Suggest how being working class might cause a high crime rate.
b) Suggest how a third factor might cause this correlation

A a) Working-class people have fewer qualifications and opportunities to succeed. As a result, they may be more likely to turn to crime to improve their situation.

b) Working-class crimes such as street crime and burglary are easier to detect than middle class crimes such as fraud. The correlation is due to a third factor – ease of detection.

OR

The police discriminate against the working class and arrest a higher proportion. They see working-class people as prone to crime. However, middle-class people may be equally prone.

TESTING HYPOTHESES

QUESTIONS AND ANSWERS

Q1   How is Rosenthal and Jacobson's hypothesis related to the self-fulfilling prophecy theory?

A   The theory states that the expectations of others will influence a person's actions. It follows from this that teachers' expectations of children's ability will affect their progress.

Q2   How did the teachers respond to the pupils they believed to be in the top 20%?

A   They gave these children 'challenging tasks' and 'special attention'. They expected more from them and thought they would make greater progress than the other 80%.

Q3   How might this response account for the children's gains in IQ?

A   If Rosenthal and Jacobson's explanation is correct, the top 20% picked up on the teachers' expectations of their ability and potential, and tended to act in terms of these expectations. This led to a self-fulfilling prophecy.

BACKGROUND

Although there has been some support for Rosenthal and Jacobson's findings, not all studies have produced similar results. Rosenthal and Jacobson's methodology has been questioned. Critics claim the IQ tests they used were of poor quality and not properly administered (Nash, 1976). The main criticism of Rosenthal and Jacobson's research (and nearly all expectation research) is the failure to conduct a detailed study of the interaction which may have led to the changes in behaviour. Rosenthal and Jacobson offered suggestions for changes in the children's behaviour but they did not actually observe teacher-pupil interaction in the classroom. They did not provide direct evidence of teachers' expectations being translated into pupil behaviour (Rist, 2007).

REFERENCES

Nash, R. (1976) *Teacher expectations and pupil learning.* London: Routledge & Kegan Paul.

Rist R.C. (2007) On understanding the processes of schooling: The contributions of labelling theory. In A.R. Sadovnik (ed.), *Sociology of education: A critical reader.* New York: Routledge, Taylor Francis Group.

QUESTIONS AND ANSWERS

Q1 *Suggest how the various factors may have contributed to the decline of crime in the USA.*

A **Zero tolerance policing.** Supporters of this approach argue that clamping down on all crimes, however insignificant, will reduce crime across the board. Widespread petty crime creates an atmosphere of lawlessness which encourages both minor and major crimes.
Note: In some cities zero tolerance policing appeared to have little effect on the crime rate, in other cities such as New York, it may have helped to reduce crime. However, some cities which did not introduce zero tolerance had similar crime reductions to cities like New York where zero tolerance appeared to work.

Economic growth and employment. Some researchers argue that economic growth contributes to crime reduction as fewer people will turn to crime in order to raise their living standards and 'succeed'. Economic growth is usually accompanied by job creation and a reduction in unemployment. Again, this is seen to reduce the pressure to turn to crime.
Note: There is no necessary connection between the state of the economy and the crime rate. Crime rates were relatively low during the Great Depression in the 1930s.

High risk age group. The decrease in the proportion of 15-29 year olds – the group with the highest crime rate – has been given as a reason for crime reduction. This view is based on the simple argument that if there are fewer high-risk young people, there will be less crime.

Police numbers. This argument is simple and simplistic – the more police, the less crime.
Note: In *Police for the Future*, David Bayley (1994), a leading expert on US police, states: 'Repeated analysis has consistently failed to find any connection between the numbers of police officers and crime rates'. At best, increases in police numbers have played only a small part in the decline in crime.

Prison. Sending more people to prison and giving them longer sentences is seen as a way of keeping potential criminals behind bars and off the streets. In terms of this argument, prison prevents them from committing crimes in the wider society. It therefore contributes to the decline of crime.

Gun control. Here, the argument states that stricter gun controls will result in fewer handgun homicides. This may have happened in northern cities like Washington D.C. and New York. However, a similar decline in handgun homicides occurred in cities like Houston, Texas, where it was much easier to buy guns.

Crack cocaine. This theory argues that the reduction in the demand for crack cocaine in the mid-1990s led to a decline in violent crime.
Note: There is a correlation between these two factors. However, it is not clear that one causes the other.

Target hardening. There is evidence that the increase in target hardening paralleled the decline in crime. However, it is not clear that one causes the other.

BACKGROUND

Some of the background material has been provided in the above 'Notes'. Clearly, the great crime decline is due to a number of factors and various combinations of those factors in different places and at different times.

But, has there been a real crime decline? Is it simply a reflection of changes in the way the statistics have been collected and analysed? First, police reporting methods did not change. Second, statistical reports on homicide and car theft from sources other than the police show a similar overall decline. According to Franklin E. Zimring (2007) in his book *The Great American Crime Decline*, 'The crime decline was real'.

QUESTIONS AND ANSWERS

Q1   Suggest reasons why the life history method allowed Mike Maguire to 'probe much more deeply than one-off interviews'?

A   First, because Maguire used a series of interviews. Second, because he got to know the burglar and probably gained his trust and friendship. This would mean he could probe more deeply without causing offence. And it would mean he would be trusted with information which would not be revealed to a stranger or to someone in authority.

Q2   Why was the life history of John Stands In Timber so important?

A   Because it provided an insider's view of the traditional way of life of the Cheyenne. And he was one of the last people to have actually lived this way of life.

Q3   Why is a case study of a particular community important?

A   A case study gives an overall picture of a community. This allows the researcher to see what's important to the people that live there and to see what people both say and do. Although it's not possible to generalise from a case study, it can provide relevant data for a large-scale questionnaire survey.

Q4   Researchers were present before and after the prophecy failed. This is the first properly observed study which has observed this process. Why is it important?

A   As the researchers state, there have been lots of 'unfulfilled prophesies and disappointed messiahs'. This is the first closely observed and detailed study of the process. In some respects, it helps us to understand the sketchy reports of such movements. And since they are a regular occurrence, historically and globally, this understanding is important.

BACKGROUND

Mike Maguire's interviewee was serving a long prison sentence. He prepared for Maguire's visits to the prison by writing notes. Each interview covered a different period of his life.

John Stands In Timber was recognised as their own historian by the Cheyenne. The importance of his life history can be seen from Margot Liberty's comments. First, 'John's narrative provides white readers with a rare insight into the history and culture of his people. With one foot in the Indian world and the other in the white world, he understands and can communicate with both'. And second, 'John has given us a history of the Cheyenne as they themselves see it'.

The Kendal research lasted six years. Kendal is a fairly self-contained community – the three nearest towns are 10 to 25 miles away. Most people would conduct their religious or spiritual lives in or near Kendal. The researchers thanked the townspeople for giving them 'access to their churches, chapels, meeting houses, centres, groups, practice rooms, shops and homes. They gave generously of their time, and spoke frankly and openly about matters of personal significance.'

In *When Prophecy Fails*, several researchers joined The Seekers as participant observers. Their investigation was 'conducted without either the knowledge or consent of the group members'. This raises ethical questions. The researchers claim that they could not conduct the study unless they kept their reasons secret. However, they admit that because they were seen as members of The Seekers, they influenced the behaviour of the group.

LONGITUDINAL STUDIES

QUESTIONS AND ANSWERS

Q1 *Why use longitudinal studies to help us to understand the class system?*

A Longitudinal studies look at the same people over time. They identify trends and processes, continuity and change. The pictures show how a person's class position at birth can shape the rest of their life. In general, the higher their class position, the greater the likelihood that they will have high educational qualifications, a well-paid job, that they will own their house and an expensive car.

In many cases, their chances of obtaining desirable things (good health, holidays) and avoiding undesirable things (longstanding illness and inability to afford holidays) are influenced by class. In general, the higher a person's class position, the better their *life chances*.

These are important findings. We need to see the cumulative effects of class. We need information about social inequality and social mobility. If we want to move towards equality of opportunity we need to see to what degree class is a barrier to this goal.

Q2 *Why is it important to look at illegal drug use over time?*

A Young people's attitudes towards and use of illegal drugs are not static, they change and develop over time. This is why longitudinal research is particularly useful to study this topic. Howard Parker's study is entitled *Illegal Leisure: The normalisation of adolescent recreational drug use.* Normalisation is a process – it means becoming normal over time. Again, longitudinal study is a particularly useful method to examine this process.

BACKGROUND

Now We Are 50: Key findings from the National Child Development Study, summary report, provides an overall picture of the first 50 years of the National Child Development Study. In the preface, Polly Toynbee describes it as 'one of the crown jewels of social research. Nothing comes close in value to the mighty British longitudinal surveys that track cohorts of babies, observing almost everything that happens to individuals throughout their lives. The most pressing political and social questions are revealed in the stories of their lives so far.'

Illegal Leisure is a powerful antidote to the often one-sided political discourse which has, in Parker's words, '… an energy of its own. This discourse promotes public fear and anxiety about crime, drugs and youth, which in turn it then uses to interfere simplistically, and with apparent public consent, in drugs and criminal justice policy and practice. This process, because it can barely be challenged, thus spins along reinforcing itself.'

A follow-up study, *Illegal Leisure Revisited* (Judith Aldridge et al, 2011), looks at the same group at age 22 and 27.

22   SOCIOLOGY IN PICTURES

OFFICIAL STATISTICS

QUESTIONS AND ANSWERS

Q1 *Why is it important to know how official statistics are constructed and used?*

A a) The first picture shows the priorities of three chief constables. In each area, these priorities may result in more rapes, street crimes and burglaries being recorded by the police as they focus on these offences. Researchers must not assume that a rise in particular recorded crimes means an actual rise in these crimes. It may simply reflect changing police priorities.

b) The second picture shows a man being interviewed as part of the annual British Crime Survey. This is a large-scale victim study. It excludes so-called 'victimless crimes' such as illegal drug possession and fraud – for example, tax evasion. However, it includes crimes not reported to the police, so for many crimes it probably gives a more accurate picture of numbers and trends than police recorded crime.

c) When governments record a rise or fall in unemployment, house building, entry into higher education, cigarette smoking and so on, it is important to know how these things are measured. For example, the changes in unemployment may simply reflect changes in the definition and measurement of unemployment, as Picture 3 suggests.

d) When political parties use statistical evidence to attack other parties, the accuracy of that evidence must be questioned. In Picture 4 the Conservative Party is using a rise in the official rate of violent crime to attack the Labour Party. However, at least part of that rise was due to a change in police methods of recording violent crime.

BACKGROUND

Despite problems with the construction and use of official statistics, they can be extremely valuable. Many government surveys are well-planned, with detailed self-completion questionnaires or structured interviews and large, representative samples. Surveys are often conducted regularly which can allow for comparisons over time and the identification of trends.

But, decisions about what statistics are collected and published are political. For example, Muriel Nissel, the first editor of *Social Trends*, an annual publication of the Office for National Statistics has written, 'From time to time, there has been great pressure on directors of statistics in departments to withhold or modify statistics, particularly in relation to employment and health, and professional integrity has forced some to threaten resignation (quoted in M.Nissel, Vital Statistics, *New Statesman*, 27th January, 1995).

STATISTICS ARE IMPORTANT

QUESTIONS AND ANSWERS

Q1 *How do the statistics on stop and search help to explain the views expressed in the pictures?*

A The statistics show that the 7:1 black:white ratio for stop and search is disproportionate. It is seen as such by many black people. They see themselves as discriminated against as the quotes in the pictures indicate.

The interviewees in *Reading the Riots* interpret this disproportion in the following way. The police are racist. They hold negative stereotypes of black people, especially young black males. They see them as potential criminals and associate them with drugs, knives and violent street crime. As a result, they often talk to young blacks as if they were 'hoodlums'.

Much of the hostility towards the police is due to the frequency of stop and search and the way it is conducted. This was given as a major reason for the riots. The police are hated by many young blacks for what is seen as unjust behaviour, for humiliating them, and for being the 'biggest gang out there'. Attacking the police is seen by some as 'payback', as 'getting back on 'em'.

BACKGROUND

Reading the Riots is a research project conducted jointly by the Guardian newspaper and the London School of Economics.

In 2010 the Equality and Human Rights Commission published a detailed examination of stop and search entitled, *Stop and Think: A critical review of the use of stop and search powers in England and Wales*. It concluded that:

'The evidence points to racial discrimination being a significant reason why in many areas of the country people from ethnic minority communities, black people in particular, are so much more likely to be stopped and searched by the police than their white neighbours. It implies, in other words, that stop and search powers are being used in a discriminatory and unlawful way. This is despite the evidence from both Staffordshire and Cleveland which proves that a reduction in the use of stop and search can go hand in hand with a reduction in the overall levels of crime. Staffordshire and Cleveland show that policing which respects human rights is more effective and actually makes us safer.'

QUESTIONS AND ANSWERS

Q1 *Judging by the first picture, why forge documents?*

A Money. In this case the forgers were paid $4 million.

Q2 *Why is there a tendency to distort when people write their memoirs or autobiographies?*

A To present themselves in the best possible light, especially when they have been publicly criticised as in the case of George W. Bush.

Q3 *Why is it important to know whether a document is representative or a one-off?*

A If a document is representative, it will tend to reflect the views of a section of the population or the whole population. If it's a one-off it may only reflect the views of an individual or a small minority. For a sociologist studying society, this is important information.

Q4 *Are the newspaper headlines representative?*

A From the information here, they appear to be representative of British tabloid newspapers over the years and may well reflect the views of their audiences.

Q5 *Why is meaning so important when interpreting documents?*

A First, researchers need to know what the document means to those who produced it and to those who see, read or hear it. This is essential if researchers are examining people's perspectives, outlooks and values. It is also important to be aware that the same thing can mean different things to different people. For example, a Jay-Z rap will probably mean somewhat different things to an African-American and a white English person. Also, the researcher needs to be aware of their own meanings and to guard against imposing them on the document.

BACKGROUND

A number of reputable historians believed that the forged Hitler diaries were genuine. At last, they thought, they had a detailed personal record written by one of the most infamous and significant figures of the 20th century.

Here are extracts from reviews of George W. Bush's memoirs, *Decision Points*.

'Very few of its 493 pages are not self-serving' (*New Yorker*, 29.11.2010).

'It is a book which is part spin, part mea culpa, part family scrapbook, part self-conscious effort to (re)shape his political legacy' (*New York Times*, 04.11.2010).

The quotes from Jay-Z are taken from his book *Decoded* (2010) in which he decodes and spells out the meaning of his lyrics. In his words:

'Rap is at heart an art form that gave voice to a specific experience, but, like every art, is ultimately about the most common human experiences: joy, pain, fear, desire, uncertainty, hope, anger, love.'

EXCHANGING NOTES

QUESTIONS AND ANSWERS

Q1   What do the girls' notes indicate about their concerns?

A   Since 90 % of what they wrote was about their relationships with each other, this seemed to be a major concern.

'Does she still like me?' and 'Will I be invited to her party?' indicate a preoccupation with friendship and popularity and a certain unease about the durability of their friendships and their standing in the peer group.

Q2   Why do the teacher and Valerie Hey have different views about the value of the girls' notes?

A   The teacher refers to the notes as 'little pieces of garbage'. The impression given here is of silly little girls writing silly little notes of no interest or value. Since the girls should be paying attention and working in lessons, writing notes probably adds to her negative view.

To Valerie Hey the notes are very valuable. She is investigating girls' friendship patterns. Here is the real thing – notes about friendship written and exchanged by the girls. The notes are not 'second hand' data from questionnaires and interviews, they are not researcher's perceptions derived from participant observation. They are 'first hand' and direct expressions and concerns about friendship which are 'untouched' by the researcher.

Q3   Why is Valerie Hey worried about the ethics of using the notes?

A   First, the notes were private. Second, in most cases, she did not have permission to use them. Third, most of the girls did not know she had possession of and had read the notes. As a result, she sometimes felt 'like a thief' and 'like a spy'.

BACKGROUND

In Valerie Hey's words, the notes provided 'visible evidence of the extensive emotional labour invested by the girls in their friendships'. They reflected the themes that emerged from her research – the girls' 'intimacy, secrecy and struggle'. They illustrated how the girls were 'intensely preoccupied by the micro-politics of their relationships', they revealed their 'passionate fallouts' and their 'sense of unease about friendships'.

Hey used a 'mixed method' approach. She combined documentary research (analysing the notes) with participant observation, case studies of several girls' networks, informal interviews, discussions in the playground, cafeteria and park, and diaries completed by some of the girls in which they recorded their social activities for a week.

RELIABILITY AND VALIDITY

QUESTIONS AND ANSWERS

Q1 **Look at the first picture. Why is the man's statement reliable but not valid?**

A The statement is reliable because if he or somebody else made the same observation, they would get the same result. However, it is not valid because the conclusion he draws from the observation is incorrect – the sun does not go round the earth.

Q2 **Why are the results of the IQ test invalid?**

A The test is not measuring what it is supposed to be measuring – the IQ of the two children. To some extent, the results reflect the differences in their culture. The Yakima girl does not finish and this lowers her score. She does not finish because her culture places little importance on speed. As a result, the test is not a valid measure of her intelligence.

Q3 **It is very unlikely that two observers will see and record the same things. Briefly comment using Redfield's and Lewis's observations?**

A There was a gap of 17 years between Redfield's and Lewis's study of Tepoztlan. Part of the difference between their observations is probably due to changes that occurred during these years. However, both researchers believe that the main reason for the difference is due to their different personalities and outlooks, which coloured their views. This indicates that their observations are not reliable and, at best, only partly valid.

BACKGROUND

It is difficult to reach firm conclusions about reliability and validity because the terms have been defined in a number of different ways. And some researchers identify different types of reliability and validity (see *Social Research Methods* by Alan Bryman, 2008).

Here are some views on the reliability and validity of data derived from different research methods. To some extent they reflect preferences for different methods.

Laboratory experiments are often seen as the most reliable because the variables can be largely controlled. However, many researchers see them as the least valid because the laboratory situation is artificial.

Participant observation has been seen by its supporters as the best chance of producing valid data because it observes people in their normal social settings. However, it is sometimes seen as especially unreliable because no two observers see things in the same way. And it is not possible to reproduce the same settings in order to repeat and test previous observations.

Official statistics are often seen as unreliable because of changes in the way things are defined and measured. For example, definitions of poverty and unemployment have changed over the years so it is not possible to compare like with like.

Questionnaire surveys based on representative samples are usually seen as fairly reliable. They can be replicated (repeated) using the same sampling method with the same questionnaire. However, some researchers query the validity of the data, arguing that people cannot express their feelings and beliefs in their own way.

Structured interviews are often seen as more reliable but less valid than unstructured interviews. In an unstructured interview, people have more opportunity to spell out their opinions and values and express their feelings in their own way. However, structured interviews are seen as more reliable because all interviewees are responding to the same set of questions.

SOCIAL FACTS

QUESTIONS AND ANSWERS

Q1 *Use Durkheim's theory to explain why those in each left-hand picture have a higher suicide rate than those in each right-hand picture.*

A **Pictures 1 and 2** Compared to a married couple, a single person is more likely to live alone and to have no special person to turn to. They are more socially isolated. As a result, there is less pressure to prevent them from taking their own life.

Pictures 3 and 4 Compared to a married couple with children, a childless married couple are less likely to form a close-knit group. Their level of social integration will be lower and therefore they will be more prone to suicide.

Pictures 5 and 6 Older adults are less integrated into the wider society than younger adults. They tend to retreat into their own company and to have a smaller social network. As a result, they will experience less pressure against suicide.

Pictures 7 and 8 People living in cities often encounter strangers in streets and shops. In this respect, they are anonymous, alone and isolated. In village communities, people often meet people they know on the street, in shops and in pubs. City dwellers are therefore more likely to have lower social integration and a higher suicide rate.

Pictures 9 and 10 According to Durkeim, Protestants tend to act as individuals in religious contexts. By comparison, Catholics tend to experience religion more as a member of a group. In this respect, Protestants are less integrated into a religious group. As a result, there is less pressure to prevent them from taking their own lives.

Pictures 11 and 12 A common enemy tends to unite a group and strengthen social bonds. This happens when a nation is at war – the level of social integration is higher. In peacetime, social bonds are weaker and the level of social integration is lower. As a result, the suicide level is higher than during a war.

BACKGROUND

Emile Durkeim (1858-1917) is one of the founders of sociology. His book *Suicide: A Study in Sociology*, first published in 1897, defined an approach to the study of society. He began by stating, 'Consider social facts as things'. Social facts are external to the individual and exercise constraint over them. Durkheim claimed that his study of suicide showed that this was the case. The level of social integration and the suicide rate are both social facts. In this case, the level of social integration exercises constraint and shapes the suicide rate.

Durkeim's study of suicide has been criticised in various ways. For example, the accuracy of the statistics on suicide he used is questionable. However, his approach remains influential.

SOCIAL CONSTRUCTION

QUESTIONS AND ANSWERS

Q1 *How does the idea of social construction differ from the idea of social facts?*

A Social construction is about the construction of meanings. These meanings form social reality – they produce a world of sense and significance. The job of the sociologist is to uncover these meanings in order to discover the social reality they create.

On the other hand, social facts are not simply meanings, they are objective things which have been caused by other objective things – by other social facts. Social facts constrain behaviour. The job of the sociologist is to identify social facts and find out what causes what.

In terms of suicide, a social construction view states that the job of the sociologist is to discover the meanings used to classify and categorise deaths as suicide. This is the approach Atkinson takes in *Discovering Suicide*. However, in *Suicide: A Study in Sociology*, Durkheim argues that sociologists should identify the social facts which cause variations in suicide rates and provide an explanation for these causal relationships.

Q2 *What is a 'typical suicide death'?*

A In this context, it is a way of ending life which is seen as typical of those who commit suicide. Examples include a drug overdose, hanging, gassing and drowning.

Q3 *What is a 'typical suicide biography'?*

A In this context, it is a biography or life history which is seen to be typical of those who commit suicide. Aspects of a 'typical suicide biography' might include divorce, lack of friends and a history of depression.

Q4 *Why is the woman in Picture 4 suggesting that the researcher is simply 'uncovering the meanings that coroners use to categorise suicide'?*

A She is suggesting that coroners are more likely to categorise deaths as suicide if the deceased has a 'typical suicide biography'. This biography contains various things which can be classified as social isolation, for example few, if any, friends. The researcher finds this out when he examines the dead person's background and assumes that this was the cause of their apparent suicide. Instead, the person's background may have been the reason why the coroner defined their death as suicide – because they have a 'typical suicide biography'. This is why the woman is suggesting that the researcher is simply uncovering the meanings used by coroners to classify a death as suicide.

BACKGROUND

There are a number of perspectives in sociology which emphasise meanings. They go under various names and often overlap. They include phenomenology, interpretivism, social constructionism, symbolic interactionism and social action theory. At one extreme, phenomenology states we live in a world of meaning. The job of the sociologist is to discover those meanings. Meanings constitute social reality, there is nothing more. At the other extreme, social action theory accepts that meanings are important, but argues that they can direct action and cause changes in society.

QUESTIONS AND ANSWERS

Q1   *How do data in numbers, measurement, questionnaires, representative samples, correlations and causal relationships fit together?*

A   Quantitative data is needed for accurate measurement. In particular, it is needed to measure the strength of relationships between various factors and to establish correlations and possible causation. A questionnaire survey based on a representative sample is the simplest and cheapest way of collecting quantitative data. This data can be used for making generalisations and establishing possible causes.

Q2   *How do qualitative data, observation and in-depth interviews fit together in the search for meaning?*

A   Observation provides the researcher with an opportunity to interpret meanings in context. In-depth interviews allow the interviewee to spell out and qualify their meanings in their own words. They allow the researcher to discuss, probe for and analyse meaning with the interviewee. Qualitative data from these sources are usually seen as 'richer' and 'deeper' than the quantitative data from questionnaire surveys.

Q3   *Look at the last picture. Does he have to choose?*

A   Most sociologists would probably say 'no'. They recognise the strengths and weaknesses of different methods and types of data. They often mix different methods and different kinds of data. They usually select particular methods to suit the type of data they require for a particular study.

BACKGROUND

Ray Pawson (1989) has strongly attacked the idea of 'two sociologies'. He argues that it gives a false impression of the relationship between theory, research methods and the actual practice of doing sociology. In his view there is a whole range of different views and different assumptions about doing research.

STARTING OUT

QUESTIONS AND ANSWERS

Q1 Why begin with library research?

A
- To bring yourself up to date with relevant books and journal articles.
- To get new ideas which may shape your research.
- To look at the methods used in existing studies to see which might be appropriate for your research.
- To develop the findings of previous research in the area.
- To make sure you don't re-invent the wheel.

Q2 Why is Kate being introduced in the school assembly?

A
- To make the whole school aware that she has come to study what the pupils eat for lunch and the reasons for their choices.
- To show that she has the head teacher's approval for her research
- To follow the British Sociological Association's ethical guidelines, which state that people should be told they are participating in research and what the research is about.

Q3 Why does she join the kitchen staff and serve the pupils?

A
- Participant observation allows her to observe the choices made by the pupils.
- It also allows her to observe the servers to see if they try to influence pupils' choices.

Q4 Why did Kate interview the head teacher, the cook and the local authority school meals' supervisor?

A
- Because they are major players in deciding school meals policy.
- This policy shapes the menu from which pupils choose their meals.

Q5 Why give the pupils a simple questionnaire to complete?

A
- To ask straightforward questions which can be answered by ticking boxes – for example, 'Do you eat fruit as part of your school lunch?.
- To provide quantitative data on questions such a gender and age.

Q6 Why discuss school meals with parents?

A
- Because they have a major say in whether the pupils have school meals or packed lunches.
- To find out their thoughts on school meals.
- To gauge their influence on school meals policy.

CHOOSING A TOPIC

QUESTIONS AND ANSWERS

Q1   **Why did Ann Oakley choose to study housework?**

A   As a feminist, Ann Oakley was concerned with women's issues, in particular women's traditional roles which she saw as limiting and oppressive. She rejected the view that a woman's place was in the home and described housework as 'work directly opposed to the possibility of human self-actualisation'. She wanted to raise awareness about women's issues and her book, *Housewife: High Value – Low Cost* (1974) did just that.

Q2   **Why did Peter Townsend spend over 50 years studying poverty?**

A   Peter Townsend was driven by his convictions. He saw poverty as a social evil. Fighting poverty and campaigning on behalf of the poor was his life's work. In his words, 'Social justice in an unending struggle'.

Q3   **Why is globalisation a popular research topic?**

A   The process of globalisation has speeded up in recent years with the spread of global communication networks and global financial markets. Many problems are global in scope and require global solutions, for example climate change and pollution. There is a growing awareness of the process of globalisation and its significance.

Choosing a research topic is influenced by issues of the day. The increasing recognition of globalisation and its importance accounts for its popularity as a research topic.

Q4   **What influence might funding organisations have on choosing a research topic?**

A   Research costs money. Most researchers require a grant to conduct their study. Funding organisations often limit grants to particular research areas. If the research topic does not fit their requirements, then grants will not be given. This may well influence choosing a topic. For example, if music festivals are not considered 'grantworthy', as the picture suggests, then this may lead to choosing a different topic.

BACKGROUND

Ann Oakley's *Housewife: High Value – Low Cost* (1974) 'should be compulsory reading for those people who think that a woman's place is, always was, and ever shall be, in the home' (*New Statesman*). And her *The Sociology of Housework*, ' is a unilateral, one-woman attempt to bridge the gap in the sociological literature' (*New Statesman*). At a time when no self-respecting male sociologist would consider studying housework, these books were groundbreaking. Since then Ann Oakley has written studies on women's rights, childbirth, women's health, gender in the social sciences and social policy. She has also found time to write novels and develop environmentally-friendly cleaning products.

MIXED METHODS

QUESTIONS AND ANSWERS

Q1   *How might the use of a mixed method approach have contributed to Paul Hodkinson's research?*

A   The various research methods used by Hodkinson probably gave a fuller, more rounded and richer picture than using a single method. Participant observation at the Whitby Gothic Weekend gave him first-hand experience of 'pure Goth'. In his words, this event is 'the ultimate experience in taking part in the Goth scene'.

Questionnaires provided quantitative data on factors such as age and gender. And the short answer questions resulted in 'some extremely valuable comments'.

Unstructured interviews gave Goths an opportunity to express their views in their own way. The interviews were 'open and flowing'. They provided, 'in-depth, quality information'.

Each method provides particular types of data. Together they combine to give an overall picture from various viewpoints.

BACKGROUND

In addition to the methods illustrated in pictures, Hodkinson used documentary research. He analysed Goth fanzines, websites, posters and music and examined their place in Goth subculture. Hodkinson summarises his methodology in the following quote.

> 'My aim was to conduct in-depth and thorough qualitative research on the Goth scene in Britain, in order to examine and account for the cultural form taken by the group. In particular, the focus was on the norms, meanings, motivations and social patterns of those involved. In order to achieve maximum depth and quality of information and understanding, I adopted a multi-method ethnographic approach, which included participant observation, in-depth interviews, media analysis and even a questionnaire.'

TRIANGULATION

QUESTIONS AND ANSWERS

Q1 **What research methods were used by the research team?**

A
- Participant observation in pubs.
- In-depth unstructured interviews with professionals such as social workers.
- Observing police/community meetings.
- Documentary research – analysis of local newspapers.
- Structured interviews – in a house-to-house survey.
- Focus group discussions with survey participants.
- Postal questionnaires sent to local businesses and organisations.
- Telephone interviews with businesses and organisations who agreed to take part.

Q2 **Judging from the final picture, how successful was triangulation?**

A It appeared to produce a well-rounded and relatively complete picture – 'quantitative and qualitative data' and 'different layers of social reality'. And, as a validity check, the researchers 'looked for confirmations and contradictions between those different layers'.

BACKGROUND

One of the main aims of triangulation is to check the validity and reliability of research findings. This is done by combining different research methods, and/or different types of data, and/or different researchers. If, for example, participant observation and interviews produce conflicting findings, or different researchers produce contradictory data, this raises questions about validity and reliability.

Mixed methods, multi-method approach and methodological pluralism all mean much the same thing – using a variety of methods in order to obtain a fuller and more rounded picture. However, they place less emphasis on validity checking than triangulation.

RESEARCH ETHICS

QUESTIONS AND ANSWERS

Q1   In what ways can Milgram's experiment be seen as unethical?

A   First, the participants were deceived. They were told the experiment was designed to study the effect of punishment – electric shocks – on learning. In fact, it was a study of obedience. The participants were told that the shocks were real – they were not.

Second, they were persuaded to continue with the experiment when they wished to stop.

Third, the experiment caused some of the participants considerable distress.

Q2   What can be said in Milgram's defence?

A   The motive for the experiment is worthwhile. It shows just how easy it is to get people to harm others. And, as Milgram argues, 'If one man in a white coat can get people to harm others, think what governments can command'.

Given the importance of the experiment and the moral issues it raises, some people argue that Milgram's research methods are justified. And, as Milgram says, 'I had to deceive them for the experiment to work'. Interestingly, 80 % of the participants thought the experiment was worthwhile.

Q3   In what ways can Humphreys' research methods be seen as unethical?

A   Humphreys deceived those he was observing. They had no idea he was conducting research. He assumed two false identities – first, as a 'watchqueen' and second, as an employee of the health service. In the process, he lied about his real reasons for being in the public toilet and in their homes. He invaded their privacy by tracking down their names and addresses and entering their homes under false pretences.

Q4   What can be said in Humphreys' defence?

A   As Humphreys said, he had to keep his research secret and invade the men's privacy in order to conduct his study. Whether this is sufficient justification is a matter of opinion. Humphreys claims that his research showed that the participants were not 'dangerous deviants' as portrayed by the stereotype. In fact, many of them were 'respectable' married men.

BACKGROUND

Milgram's research has been branded as unethical by his critics who see it as deliberate deception, lacking informed consent, disregarding the right to withdraw and failing to protect participants from psychological harm. Milgram defends himself on every count.

First, he argues that the importance of his findings justifies the methods he used. In his words, 'If this experiment serves to jar people out of their complacency, it will have served its end'. And, 'If an anonymous experimenter can successfully command adults to subdue a 50-year-old man and force on him painful electric shocks against his protests, one can only wonder what government, with its vastly greater authority and prestige, can command of its subjects'.

Second, Milgram admits that in some cases there was psychological harm. He quotes someone who watched the experiment. ' I observed a mature and initially poised businessman enter the laboratory smiling and confident. Within 20 minutes he was reduced to a twitching, stuttering wreck, who was rapidly approaching a point of nervous collapse.'

However, Milgram argues that these effects were only short term. He hired a psychiatrist to interview the participants one year after the experiment. There appeared to be no indication of long-term harm.

Milgram's experiment was deception from beginning to end. The participants had no chance to give informed consent. Milgram justifies this in the following way. 'Illusion is used when necessary in order to set the stage for the revelation of certain difficult-to-get-at truths.' Over 80% of the participants said they saw deception as necessary and therefore acceptable.

Milgram states, 'The central moral justification for allowing a procedure of the sort used in my experiment is that it is judged acceptable by those who have taken part in it'.

Did the participants have a right to withdraw from the experiment? Only after four commands to continue ending with, 'You have no other choice, you must go on'. Despite begging to withdraw, some obeyed these commands, though doing so caused them distress. Milgram describes one participant, 'At one point he pushed his fist into his forehead and muttered: "Oh God, let's stop it". And yet he continued to respond to every word of the experimenter, and obeyed to the end.'

It is very unlikely that ethics committees in university departments would allow Milgram's experiments to be conducted today.

Laud Humphreys admits that his research involved deceit, invasion of privacy and no opportunity for informed consent. However, as long as the confidentiality of the participants was preserved – which he claims it was – Humphreys sees his study as justified. His argument runs as follows.

The public and the police had simplistic stereotypes of gay people, particularly those involved in casual sex in public restrooms. The majority of arrests of gay men were for this behaviour. Humphreys believed that the police were wasting time and money on a relatively harmless activity and were harassing and demonising men who were often 'respected' members of the community. He argued that his research would help to destroy superficial stereotypes and provide much needed support for the men involved.

Humphreys' research showed that 54% of the men he studied were married. Only 14% were members of the gay community and mainly interested in homosexual relationships. There is anecdotal evidence which suggests that Humphreys' findings persuaded some police forces to direct their resources to what he would regard as better use. And if this is the case, Humphreys would see the so-called unethical aspects of his research as justified.